MA+H
EVERYWHERE

WHAT ARE THE CHANCES?

Probability, Statistics, **Ratios,** and **Proportions**

Rob Colson

Children's Press®
An Imprint of Scholastic Inc.

W9-BYR-610

Acknowledgments and Photo Credits

Library of Congress Cataloging-in-Publication Data
A CIP catalog record for this book is available from the Library of Congress.

No part of this publication may be reproduced in whole or in part, or stored in a retrieval system, or transmitted in any form or by any means, electronic, mechanical, photocopying, recording, or otherwise, without written permission of the publisher. For information regarding permission, write to Scholastic Inc., Attention: Permissions Department, 557 Broadway, New York, NY 10012.

Copyright © The Watts Publishing Group, 2016
First published by Franklin Watts 2016
Published in the United States by Scholastic Inc. 2018

All rights reserved.

Printed in China

SCHOLASTIC, CHILDREN'S PRESS, and associated logos are trademarks and/or registered trademarks of Scholastic Inc.

1 2 3 4 5 6 7 8 9 10 R 27 26 25 24 23 22 21 20 19 18

Photo credits:
t-top, b-bottom, l-left, r-right, c-center, front cover-fc, back cover-bc
All images courtesy of Dreamstime.com unless indicated:
Inside front Atman; fc, bc Pablo631; fcbl Jennifer Bray; bcc Rawpixelimages; 1c, 9c, 28b Ronalds Stikans; 4tl lineartestpilot/shutterstock.com; 4cr Davulcu; 4b Svanhorn4245; fccr, 5b Alexlmx; 4c Tigatelu; 7 Tijanap; bctl, 7b, 31t Dannyphoto80; 8c, 23t Mexrix; 8tb, 28t Cowpland; fccl, Valeriy Kachaev; 10t Zentilia; 11b Gorbelabda; fctr, 12l Ronstik; 13t Andrey Lobachev/Shutterstock; 13b Nikolais; fctc, 14t Hamsterman; 14tc Ha4ipuri; 14b Basheeradesigns; 16t Jenny Lipets-michaeli; 16b Rawpixelimages; 18l Evgenii Naumov; 19 Cameramannz; fctc, 20b Gilotyna; 21t Larryrains; 22b Andreadonetti; 22br Paul Michael Hughes; 23cl NASA, fcbr, 23cr Macrovector; 24c Ayo88; 26b Viteethumb; bctr, 27t Huseyin Bas; 27b Jim McMahon; 29r Binkski; 32t Stylephotographs

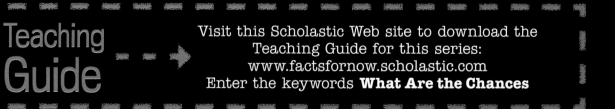

Teaching
Guide

Visit this Scholastic Web site to download the Teaching Guide for this series:
www.factsfornow.scholastic.com
Enter the keywords **What Are the Chances**

MIX
Paper from responsible sources
FSC
www.fsc.org
FSC® C104740

Luck of the **Draw**   4

Out of **100**   6

Rolling the **Dice**   8

It's a **Lottery**   10

Coins and **Cards**   12

Taking an **Average**   14

Not What It **Seems**   16

How to **Mislead** with **Statistics**   18

What's the **Ratio?**   20

The **Golden Ratio**   22

Showing Your **Final Results**   24

Election Math Around **the World**   26

Quiz   28

Glossary   31

Index, Facts for Now, and **Answers**   32

Luck of the Draw

Probability is a calculation of the chance that something will happen. Also known as odds, probability shows how often you could expect something to happen if you were to repeat it again and again. For example, you could expect to be struck by lightning once every 900,000 years.

Probable or Possible?

The chance of something happening can be expressed by a number between 0 and 1, where 0 means it will never happen, and 1 means it will happen every time. A 1-in-2 chance means that something is likely to happen exactly half the time.

Odds of being struck by lightning next year

900,000 to 1

Odds of being dealt four of a kind in poker

4,161 to 1

Odds of a mother having identical twins

285 to 1

Odds of throwing two sixes with a pair of dice

36 to 1

"You grow another nose."

"You toss a coin and get heads."

"Christmas falls on December 25."

0
(impossible)

1 in 2
(even chance)

1
(certain)

"You win the lottery jackpot."

"It rains during the World Series."

Winning Numbers

In some lotteries, players choose six different numbers between 1 and 49. To win the jackpot, these numbers must match six numbers drawn at random. There are 13,983,816 possible combinations of numbers, but only one can win. So the odds of winning are:

13,983,815 to 1

Out of 100

The percent symbol means "out of 100." It is a way of expressing a fraction in terms of parts per 100.

1% is one part in 100. Here, one square in 100 is colored red.

100% of the squares have a white outline.

25 of these 50 squares are colored green, which is 50%.

1	2	3	4	5	6	7	8	9	10
11	12	13	14	15	16	17	18	19	20
21	22	23	24	25	26	27	28	29	30
31	32	33	34	35	36	37	38	39	40
41	42	43	44	45	46	47	48	49	50
51	52	53	54	55	56	57	58	59	60
61	62	63	64	65	66	67	68	69	70
71	72	73	74	75	76	77	78	79	80
81	82	83	84	85	86	87	88	89	90
91	92	93	94	95	96	97	98	99	100

1	2	3	4	5
6	7	8	9	10
11	12	13	14	15
16	17	18	19	20
21	22	23	24	25
26	27	28	29	30
31	32	33	34	35
36	37	38	39	40
41	42	43	44	45
46	47	48	49	50

Percentages as Fractions and Decimals

Percentages as Fractions
When we say 20%, what we mean is the fraction

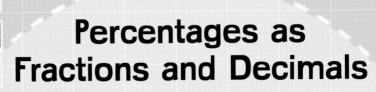

Simplifying the fraction, $20/100$ can also be expressed as $1/5$.

Percentages as Decimals
To write a percentage as a decimal, you **divide the number** by 100 by moving the decimal two places to the left:

20% becomes 0.20

Borrowers Beware!

People who borrow money from a bank are charged interest. This is additional money that you must pay back on top of the amount borrowed. If you don't pay the money back, the interest can mount up. This is due to something called **compound interest**, where interest is charged on the interest!

For example, if you borrow **$100** at an interest rate charged at **10%** at the end of each year, you will owe **$110** after the first year.

$$100 + (100 \times 10\%) = 110$$

If you think that after 10 years you'll owe $200, you've forgotten the power of compound interest.

In the second year, you are charged interest on $110, not $100. At the end of the second year, you will owe

$121
$$110 + (110 \times 10\%) = 121$$

At the end of the third year, you will owe

$133.10
$$121 + (121 \times 10\%) = 133.10$$

After 10 years, you will owe

$259.37

"I owe how much?"

Sales Talk

Shops advertise sales in a way that makes the deal seem better than it is. "Buy one, get one half price" sounds impressive, but what it really means is that you get **25%** off the price of each item when you buy two. Nothing is "half price" in that deal—everything is **75%** of the full price.

$1 + $0.50
= $1.50
= 75% × $2

Rolling the Dice

A standard die has six sides with one to six dots on each side. The chance of rolling any particular number is 1 divided by the number of sides, or $^1/_6$ (1 in 6).

Two Dice

Working out the probability of different scores with two dice is more complicated. Some scores are more likely than others. To see this, think about rolling the same die twice. Combining the scores of each roll gives possible scores of 2 to 12. There are 36 possible combinations, many of which give the same score.

Score from die two

	2	3	4	5	6	7
	3	4	5	6	7	8
	4	5	6	7	8	9
	5	6	7	8	9	10
	6	7	8	9	10	11
	7	8	9	10	11	12

Score from die one

The most likely score is 7. There are 6 different possible ways of scoring 7, which gives a probability of $^6/_{36}$, or $^1/_6$. By contrast, there is just one way to score 12: rolling a 6, then another 6. That gives a probability of $^1/_{36}$. Can you work out the probability of scoring 3?

Doubles?

The chance of throwing a double (the same number twice) is the same as the chance of throwing a particular number once: whichever number you throw first, you need that number on the second throw. The chance of that happening is $^1/_6$. The six possible doubles are in the black squares across the diagonal in the chart above.

The Game of Pig

The game of Pig is a simple two-player dice game that involves working out risk. All you need to play is a die. Player 1 rolls the die and can keep rolling until she decides to "hold" or rolls a 1. If she holds, she keeps the score of the rolls added together, but if she rolls a 1, she scores a zero. Then it is the second player's turn. The first player to get to 100 is the winner. So, for instance, if Ann rolls 4–5–1, she scores zero, or "pig," and it is then Bob's turn. If Bob then rolls 6–3 and holds, he scores 9, and it's Ann's turn again.

"Aarrgghh, pig."

"Woo-hoo, 5, then 6."

Strategies for Playing Pig

Each time you roll the die, there's a $1/6$ chance that you'll roll a 1. How many times would you risk it to get yourself a greater score? Mathematicians study games like this to explore probability and risk. There are three different factors that you need to weigh: the total for your turn, your score before your turn, and your opponent's score. If you're winning, you might take fewer risks, but if your opponent is close to 100, you may have little choice but to go for it.

It's a Lottery

In many national and state lotteries, the jackpot is several million dollars. To win the money, players must match their choice of six numbers between 1 and 49 to the numbers drawn.

Jackpot!

One way to work out the odds of winning the jackpot is to look at each choice by turn. The first choice has a $6/49$ chance of being one of the six numbers. If that number is there, then the second choice has a $5/48$ chance. If that's there, the third choice has a $4/47$ chance. The final choice has just a $1/44$ chance of being there.

So the odds of winning are:

$$6/49 \times 5/48 \times 4/47 \times 3/46 \times 2/45 \times 1/44 = 720/10,068,347,520$$

Simplifying, that works out to odds of

$$1/13,983,816$$

to win the jackpot.

Favorite Numbers

Each number has the same chance of coming up, so the odds of the numbers being 1, 2, 3, 4, 5, and 6 are the same as the odds for 3, 11, 19, 21, 36, and 43. However, if people choose numbers that others don't choose, they won't have to share the pot if they win. And it turns out that we're far from random in our selections.

The House Always Wins

There is always one winner every week in the lottery, and that is the lottery itself. State and national lotteries are set up to make money for good causes. To guarantee a profit, the lottery makes sure that the total payout each week is less than the total earned in ticket sales. In the United States, the payout for most lotteries ranges from **50 to 70%**. This means that the remaining percentage goes to the lottery, not to the winners. **The only way to guarantee a win in the lottery is to run one!**

Unlucky!

Spare a thought for a woman who played both the Maryland and Delaware state lotteries one week in 1990. Both sets of numbers came up. Unfortunately for her, her Maryland numbers came up in Delaware, and her Delaware numbers came up in Maryland, so she didn't win a penny!

Avoiding the Obvious:

1. Avoid low numbers—lots of people choose birthdays, but there are only 31 days in any month, so the numbers 32–49 are less popular.

2. Avoid 3 and 7 in particular—these are many people's favorites, as is any number ending in a 7.

3. The number 13 is thought unlucky by some, which is why it could prove very profitable for others.

4. The least popular number of all is 34. But keep that fact a secret—if too many people find out, it just might change!

Coins and Cards

"Uh-oh, I don't like heights."

Heads or Tails

The toss of a coin represents an equal chance of each outcome: it's either heads or tails. Each toss is independent, which means that you're not more likely to get tails this time just because you got heads last time.

Double or Nothing?

The chance of getting every call wrong halves with each toss. So there is a $1/2$ chance of getting one wrong, $1/4$ chance of getting two out of two wrong, $1/8$ chance of getting three out of three wrong, and $1/16$ chance of getting four out of four wrong. When betting on a coin toss, it may be worth asking "Double or nothing?" That's asking to have another toss for either twice the prize—or nothing. If someone has to ask too many times, that person is likely to end up with nothing.

But beware:

Unlikely things can happen—each time, the person is trading a chance of coming out even with a chance of a bigger loss!

Is It a Fair Toss?

After tossing a fair coin five times and coming up with five heads, the chance of a sixth heads is still $1/2$.

However, what if someone were to come up with 200 heads in a row?

The chance of 200 heads in a row is $1/2^{200}$ (2^{200} is 2 multiplied by itself 200 times). You're more likely to win the lottery every week for two months straight. When something this unlikely happens, you need to question your assumptions. You have assumed it is a fair coin, but is it really? If someone throws 200 heads in a row, ask to have a look at the coin. It probably has heads on both sides.

"Seems like cheating to me!"

Pick a Card

Card players need to know what the chances are of picking certain cards. A standard deck has 52 cards, so the chance of being dealt any one card is $1/52$. There are four aces, so the chance of being dealt an ace is $4/52$, or $1/13$.

What are the chances of being dealt two aces as your first cards?

Here, you need to remember that after the first choice, there are now only 51 cards left, and only three of them are aces. The chance of the second card being an ace is $3/51$, or $1/17$. Multiplying the chances together, you get $1/13 \times 1/17 = 1/221$.

Taking an Average

An average is a way of expressing the central value of a set of values. Mathematicians use several different ways of calculating an average.

How Tall?

The heights (in feet) of seven students in a class are as follows.

4.5, 5.9, 3.9, 6.2, 5.5, 4.5, 5.2

To calculate the **mean average height**, you add up all the heights and divide by the number of students.

$$4.5 + 5.9 + 3.9 + 6.2 + 5.5 + 4.5 + 5.2 = 35.7 \div 7 = 5.1$$

To calculate the **median height**, you line the heights up in order and take the middle value:

3.9, 4.5, 4.5, 5.2 5.5, 5.9, 6.2

So the **median height** is **5.2**.

The **mode** is the most common height. There are two students who are **4.5 feet** in height, so the mode is **4.5**. The **range** is the difference between the tallest and the shortest. Here, the range is:

$$6.2 - 3.9 = 2.3$$

6.5 feet

4.9 feet

3.2 feet

1.6 feet

A Closer Shave?

A study that followed more than 2,000 men over 20 years found that men who shaved every day lived longer, on average, than men who did not shave every day. The study was reported in the press as having found a link between shaving and a longer life. However, it does not mean that men should shave more often for their health. It only means that men who don't look after their health are also less likely to shave. As a rule, scientists say that

correlation

(things happening together) does not necessarily mean

causation

(one of the things causes the other). It could be that both things are caused by something else entirely.

Resetting the Median

IQ scores rank us according to our ability to answer questions on tests. A score of 100 is set to be the median score for the whole population. However, we are getting better at IQ tests, and every few years, the scale has to be reset— an IQ score of 100 today needs a much higher mark than it needed 50 years ago. Scientists argue over why this is. Are we getting smarter, or are we just getting better at taking tests?

Not What It Seems

We often have a feel for how likely something is. For instance, before working out the exact odds, you can have a good sense that throwing ten 6s in a row with a die is unlikely. But sometimes we can be fooled. Here is a mind-twisting example.

The Blood Test

A blood test for a certain disease can give two results:

Positive means you have the disease.

Negative means you don't have the disease.

The test is known to be **99%** accurate. This means that the test gives the wrong result once every 100 tests.

We also know that the disease is found, on average, in **1 person** out of every **10,000**.

You take the test, and the result is positive. But what are the chances that you actually have the disease?

How worried should you be?

The answer might surprise you. You have only about a **1%** chance of having the disease. There is a **99%** chance that the test was wrong!

To see why this is, imagine performing the test on

10,000 people.

On average, just one of the people will have the disease. However, 1/100 of 10,000 tests will produce false results:

$$\frac{1}{100} \times 10{,}000 = 100$$

So there are, on average, **100 false results** in every **10,000 tests**. Where the test should have identified **one person** with the disease, it in fact came up with about **100 names**. There's about a **99%** chance that your name will be one of those mistakes.

"Oh no, it's me isn't it?"

This result is known as a **"false positive,"** and it is the reason doctors often perform tests several times to confirm a diagnosis.

How to Mislead with Statistics

When you hear the word *average*, be careful that you know which average is being used. The average amount of something per person and the amount an average person has may be two very different things.

Bad Drivers

About 80% of people consider themselves to be above-average drivers. However, using the median average, exactly 50% of drivers must be below average! At least 30% of people must be wrong.

"Hey, it wasn't my fault!"

Average Apples

Here is a list of the number of apples produced by six people's gardens in a year.

Williams	350
Smith	7,000
Johnson	0
Jones	0
Gomez	150
Davis	200
Diaz	0

18

How Hot?

In a test, four diners are asked to rank three peppers by how hot they taste, with the hottest ranked third. Here are the results:

	Pepper 1	Pepper 2	Pepper 3
Ethan	3	1	2
Molly	3	2	1
Josh	3	1	2
Maria	3	2	1

The mean scores for each pepper from these results are as follows:

	Pepper 1	Pepper 2	Pepper 3
	3	1.5	1.5

Does that make pepper 1 twice as hot as peppers 2 and 3?

Everyone agrees that **pepper 1** is the **hottest**, so it is probably much hotter than **pepper 2** or **3**. It may be that it is **1,000 times hotter**. As these are rankings only, the **mean average** is only the **mean ranking** and tells us nothing about how hot the peppers actually are.

The **mean** number of apples per garden is

However, the **median** is just

and the **mode** is

1,100 150 0

It turns out that the Smiths have a whole orchard in their garden; the Williamses, Gomezes, and Davises have one tree each; and everyone else has no tree at all.

So which do you think is the "average" garden?

To avoid this kind of distortion, mean averages are sometimes taken with the highest and lowest numbers removed. Taking away the Coxes and one of the gardens that produced no apples, you get a much more sensible mean of 140.

What's the Ratio?

Ratios are a way to compare one thing to another using mathematics. A ratio is usually written in the form

a:b

Making Juice

Orange juice comes in concentrated form. To make it drinkable, you add water in a ratio of 1:3. This means that you need three parts of water for every one part of concentrate.

To make a quart of juice:

Scaling Up

Model airplane kits allow you to make a model that has exactly the same proportions as the real thing. A popular scale is **1:72**.

Life-size airplane

This scale was chosen to make the imperial measurement of **1 inch (about 2.5 cm)** on the model equivalent to exactly **6 feet (1.8 m)** on the real plane. That's about the height of a full-grown man.

6 feet

Model airplane

1 inch

1 part
concentrate
(8 oz.
concentrate)

3 parts
water
(24 oz.
water)

4 parts juice
(1 quart, or
32 oz., juice)

France

| 1 | 1 | 1 |

3 feet

Thailand

| 1 |
| 1 |
| 2 |
| 1 |
| 1 |

Flags

National flags are made using ratios. The French and Thai flags both have stripes of blue, white, and red, but the ratios are very different. The French national flag has three equal vertical bands with a 1:1:1 ratio, while the Thai flag has five horizontal bands with a 1:1:2:1:1 ratio.

Both flags have a width:length ratio of

2:3

The Golden Ratio

The golden ratio is a special number, known as phi (φ), that crops up in many places in nature and has long been used by artists and architects. It describes a proportion that we find balanced and pleasing to look at.

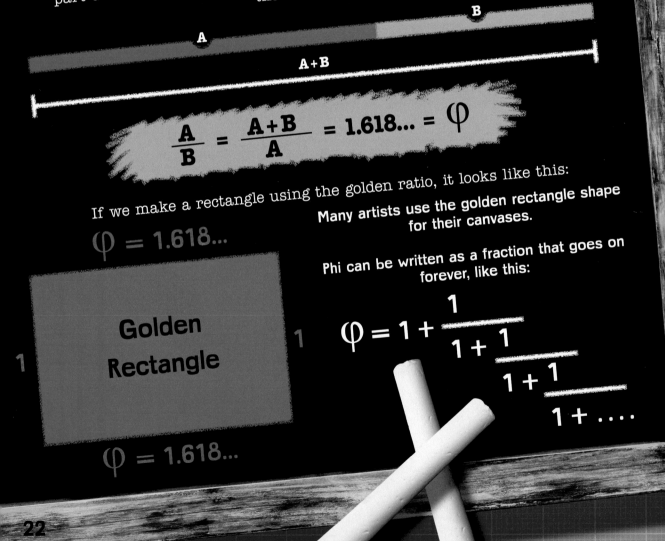

Finding the Golden Ratio

To find the golden ratio, you need to divide a line such that the longer part divided by the smaller part is equal to the whole line divided by the larger part.

A

B

A+B

$$\frac{A}{B} = \frac{A+B}{A} = 1.618... = \varphi$$

If we make a rectangle using the golden ratio, it looks like this:

$$\varphi = 1.618...$$

Golden Rectangle

$$\varphi = 1.618...$$

1

1

Many artists use the golden rectangle shape for their canvases.

Phi can be written as a fraction that goes on forever, like this:

$$\varphi = 1 + \cfrac{1}{1 + \cfrac{1}{1 + \cfrac{1}{1 + ...}}}$$

The Golden Spiral

A golden rectangle has a special property. Draw a square inside it, and you produce another golden rectangle by its side. You can keep repeating this to produce ever-smaller golden rectangles. Joining up the corners of each square, you produce a golden spiral.

The Whirlpool Galaxy's billions of stars form into golden spirals.

The seeds in a sunflower are arranged in golden spirals.

Perfect Pentagrams

A pentagram is the shape of a five-pointed star, which has been used by many human societies as a magical symbol. Does it look like a pleasing shape to you? **Three golden ratios can be found in a pentagram:**

$$a/b = 1.618$$
$$b/c = 1.618$$
$$c/d = 1.618$$

Showing Your Final Results

When faced with a mass of numbers, it can be hard to see patterns and interpret your results. Mathematicians have various ways of displaying their results, using tables, charts, and graphs.

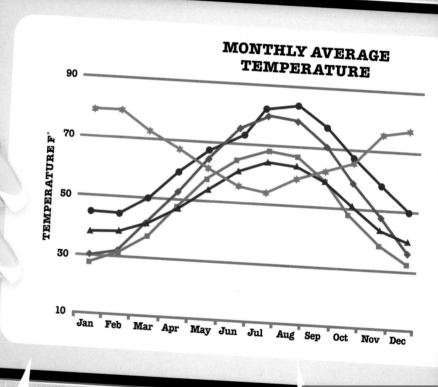

MONTHLY AVERAGE TEMPERATURE

"Brrrr, it's snowing here in New York."

"Ha-ha, we just got back from the beach in Miami!"

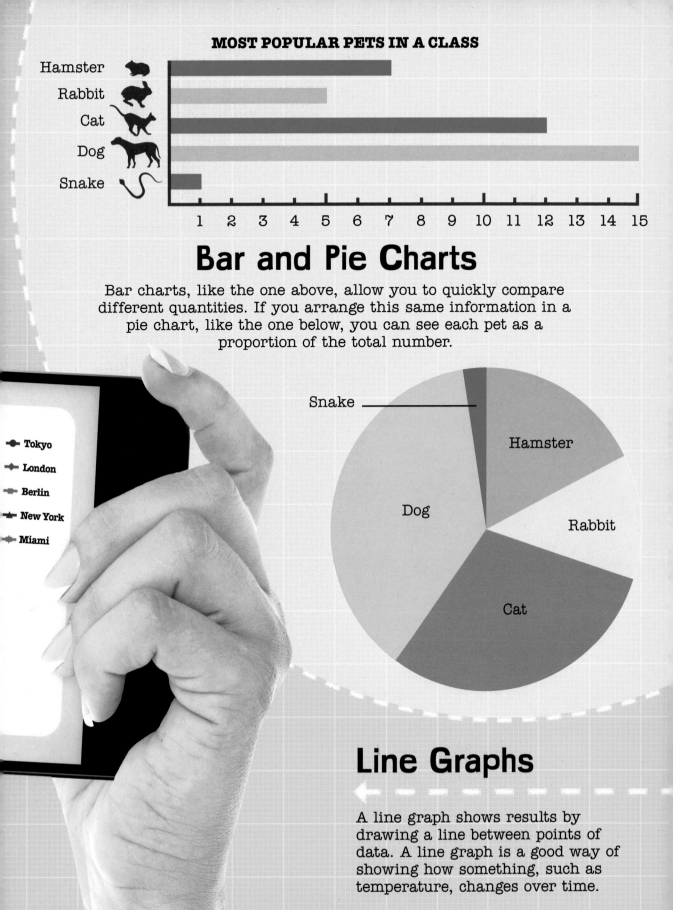

MOST POPULAR PETS IN A CLASS

Hamster
Rabbit
Cat
Dog
Snake

1 2 3 4 5 6 7 8 9 10 11 12 13 14 15

Bar and Pie Charts

Bar charts, like the one above, allow you to quickly compare different quantities. If you arrange this same information in a pie chart, like the one below, you can see each pet as a proportion of the total number.

Snake ——————

Hamster

Dog

Rabbit

Cat

- Tokyo
- London
- Berlin
- New York
- Miami

Line Graphs

A line graph shows results by drawing a line between points of data. A line graph is a good way of showing how something, such as temperature, changes over time.

Election Math Around the World

Proportional Representation

Many countries use an electoral method called proportional representation. In Italy, for example, voters vote for a party rather than an individual candidate. The party gains seats in the legislature in proportion to its share of the vote. For example, let's say that the legislature has 200 seats, that six parties are competing in the election, and that the parties receive the following shares of the vote:

In a democracy, leaders win public office through elections. Those running the election need a system to measure who is the most popular candidate or party, which isn't always as easy as it sounds. Here are some systems used around the world.

Blue	Red	Orange	Pink	Green	Purple
20%	**35%**	**6%**	**21%**	**10%**	**8%**

The parties receive seats according to the percentage of 200 that their vote represents:

Blue 40 seats, **Red** 70 seats, **Orange** 12 seats, **Pink** 42 seats, **Green** 20 seats, **Purple** 16 seats.

To form a government, a party or a coalition of parties must have a majority—that is, more than 50%—which in this case means 101 seats or more. In our example, no single party has a majority, so parties will have to form a coalition to bring their total up to at least 101. For example, Red and Pink could form a coalition, or Blue, Pink, and Green.

Countries with proportional representation often have a large number of parties because even a small party can win at least a few seats and may participate in a coalition government. Sometimes a tiny party can have great influence if its seats are needed to reach a majority.

U.S. Election Math

The United States uses an electoral method called "first past the post." In this system, each seat in the legislature is assigned to a particular district. If there are more than two candidates, the candidate with the most votes may win without having a majority. In the following example, the Blue party would win, even though it lacks a majority.

Blue	Red	Orange
45%	40%	15%

With this method, one party may win a sizable number of votes in different districts, but if it never comes in first, it will never win a seat. Some people think this is unfair. Supporters of this system say it is more likely to produce a clear winner, which makes for a stronger government.

The Electoral College

For U.S. presidential elections, states are assigned a certain number of electoral votes (see map) in the 538-vote Electoral College. Each state gets as many electoral votes as it has representatives and senators in Congress. The candidate who receives a majority (at least 270) of the electoral votes wins.

The Electoral College winner isn't always the winner of the popular vote. That's because most states give all their electoral votes to the candidate who wins the state's popular vote, regardless of the margin. The Electoral College outcome differed from the popular vote in 1888, 2000, and 2016. In each case, the candidate with the most electoral votes became president.

WASHINGTON 12
OREGON 7
MONTANA 3
IDAHO 4
NORTH DAKOTA 3
MINNESOTA 10
SOUTH DAKOTA 3
WYOMING 3
NEVADA 6
UTAH 6
COLORADO 9
NEBRASKA 5
WISCONSIN 10
IOWA 6
MICHIGAN 16
VERMONT 3
NEW HAMPSHIRE 4
MAINE 4
MASSACHUSETTS 11
NEW YORK 29
RHODE ISLAND 4
CONNECTICUT 7
PENNSYLVANIA 20
NEW JERSEY 14
ILLINOIS 20
INDIANA 11
OHIO 18
WEST VIRGINIA 5
VIRGINIA 13
DELAWARE 3
MARYLAND 10
CALIFORNIA 55
ARIZONA 11
NEW MEXICO 5
KANSAS 6
MISSOURI 10
KENTUCKY 8
NORTH CAROLINA 15
OKLAHOMA 7
ARKANSAS 6
TENNESSEE 11
SOUTH CAROLINA 9
WASHINGTON, D.C. 3
ALABAMA 9
GEORGIA 16
MISSISSIPPI 6
ALASKA 3
HAWAII 4
TEXAS 38
LOUISIANA 8
FLORIDA 29

Alaska and Hawaii are not drawn to scale or placed in their proper geographic positions.

Quiz

1 What **percentage** of these squares is colored yellow?

a)

1	2	3	4	5	6	7	8	9	10
11	12	13	14	15	16	17	18	19	20
21	22	23	24	25	26	27	28	29	30
31	32	33	34	35	36	37	38	39	40
41	42	43	44	45	46	47	48	49	50
51	52	53	54	55	56	57	58	59	60
61	62	63	64	65	66	67	68	69	70
71	72	73	74	75	76	77	78	79	80
81	82	83	84	85	86	87	88	89	90
91	92	93	94	95	96	97	98	99	100

b)

1	2	3	4	5	6	7	8	9	10
11	12	13	14	15	16	17	18	19	20
21	22	23	24	25	26	27	28	29	30
31	32	33	34	35	36	37	38	39	40
41	42	43	44	45	46	47	48	49	50
51	52	53	54	55	56	57	58	59	60

c)

1	2	3	4	5	6	7	8

2 Express each of the above percentages as a **fraction** in its simplest form.

3 Rolling **two fair dice**, what are the chances of rolling

a) **double 1**

b) **3 and 4**

c) **a total of 10 or more**

4 In a lottery, you win the jackpot if you choose **six numbers out of 49 correctly.**

You are watching the drawing take place, and your first five numbers all come up. **What are the chances** that you will win the jackpot when the **last ball** is drawn?

5 In three coin tosses, what are the chances of throwing **two heads** and **a tail**?

6 You choose **two cards** at random from a standard deck. What are the chances that they are both the

same suit?

7 Look at these exam results for a math class.

83 42 55 69 12 94 65

a) What is the **mean average** score?
b) What is the **median score**?

8 a) What is the **mode** out of these numbers?

2 4 3 3 5 6 5 3 7 3

b) If you choose a number **at random** from the list, what are the chances that it will be the **mode value**?

9 A model aircraft is made to a scale of **1:50**. If its wingspan in real life is **65 feet**, what is the wingspan of the model in inches?

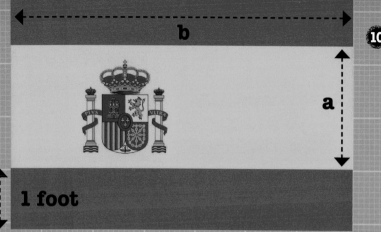

This is the flag of
Spain. The proportions
of the stripes are in
the **ratio 1:2:1**. The
proportions of the
width to length are
in the **ratio 2:3**. What
are the measurements
of **a** and **b**?

11 We asked **60 children**
how they traveled to school. The
answers were as follows: **bus
17, on foot 11, bicycle 8, car 20,
train 4**. Which pie chart shows
this correctly?

12 In an election using the
proportional representation
system, the following
percentage votes were won
by each party: **Blue 5, Red 11,
Orange 33, Pink 36, Green 15**.
The two parties with the
highest percentages, Pink and
Orange, are asked to try to
form a coalition government
with at least **51%** of the vote.
They refuse to form a coalition
with each other and want to
form coalitions with as few
other parties as possible.

a) What **coalitions** could the
parties form that would give
them a **majority**?
b) If the Blue party refuses to
ally with the Red party and
the Green party refuses to ally
with the Orange party, **which
coalition** will be formed?

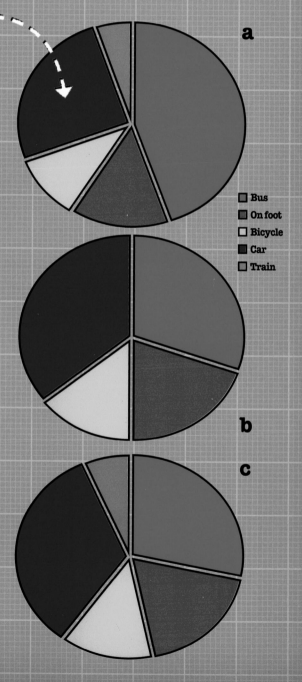

a

Bus
On foot
Bicycle
Car
Train

b

c

Glossary

Bar chart
A way of displaying results in which the length of the bar is proportional to the value it represents.

False positive
A result in a medical test that incorrectly indicates that a certain disease or condition is present.

Golden ratio
A special ratio between two lengths, in which dividing the sum of the lengths by the longer length produces the same number as dividing the longer length by the shorter length. Also called phi (φ), it is equal to approximately 1.618.

Line graph
A way of displaying results in which each data point is connected to the one next to it by a straight line. A line graph can be useful in seeing how a value changes over time.

Mean
An average that is found by adding a set of values together, then dividing by the number of values.

Median
An average that is the middle value of a set of values arranged in order. Half the remaining values are larger than the median, half are smaller.

Mode
An average that is the most frequent value in a set of values.

Payout
In a lottery, the percentage of the total amount paid for tickets that is given out in prize money.

Percentage
A fraction that is expressed in terms of parts per 100.

Pie chart
A circular chart divided into parts (shaped like pieces of pie) so that the size of each part represents the relative quantity or frequency of something.

Probability
The chance that something will happen. Probabilities can be expressed in various ways: as a fraction between 0 and 1; as a ratio of the number of times the thing will happen to the number of times it will not happen; or as a percentage. For instance, the chance of throwing heads with a fair coin toss can be written as ½, 1:1, or 50%.

Proportional representation
A way of running an election in which each party receives seats in a legislative body according to the percentage of the vote it receives.

Range
The difference between the largest and smallest values in a set of values.

Ratio
The relationship in quantity, amount, or size between two or more things.

Index

assumptions 13
averages 14–15

bar charts 25

cards 13
causation 15
charts 24–25
coalition
  government 27
coin toss 12–13
compound interest 7
correlation 15

decimal 6
democracy 26
dice 4, 8–9
doubles (dice) 8

elections 26–27
Electoral College 27
even chance 4

false positive 17
first past the post
  (elections) 27
flags 21
fraction 6

golden ratio 22–23
golden rectangle
  22–23
golden spiral 23
graphs 24–25

identical twins 4
imperial
  measurements 20

interest 7
IQ tests 15

jackpot 5, 10

lightning strike 4
line graphs 24–25
lottery 5, 10–11

mean 14, 15, 19
median 14, 15,
  18, 19
mode 14, 19

odds 4–5, 10

payout 11
pentagram 23
percentage 6–7

phi (φ) 22–23
pie charts 25
Pig (game of) 9
poker 4
probability 4–5
proportional
  representation 26

range 14
ranking 19
ratios 20–21

sales 7
scale 20
sunflower 23

Whirlpool Galaxy 23

Facts for Now

Visit this Scholastic Web site for more information on probability and statistics and to download the Teaching Guide for this series:
www.factsfornow.scholastic.com
Enter the keywords **What Are the Chances**

Answers

1. a) 20% b) 40% c) 75%
2. a) $^1/_5$ b) $^2/_5$ c) $^3/_4$
3. a) $^1/_{36}$ b) $^1/_{18}$ c) $^1/_6$
4. There is a $^1/_{44}$ chance that your sixth number will be drawn, so the chance of winning the jackpot is $^1/_{44}$.
5. There are three different ways you can do this: tails first, tails second, or tails third. Overall, there are 2 × 2 × 2 possible combinations, so the chance of two heads and one tails is $^3/_8$.
6. There are 13 of each suit in the deck. Whichever card you pick first, there are now 12 of the same suit left in a pack of 51 cards. So the chance that both cards are the same suit is $^{12}/_{51}$.
7. a) 60 b) 65
8. a) The mode is 3. b) 3 occurs 4 times out of 10, so the chance of picking the mode is $^4/_{10}$, or $^2/_5$.
9. 65 feet = 780 inches; 780 inches ÷ 50 = 15.6 inches
10. a) 2 feet b) 6 feet
11. c
12. a) Pink/Green; Pink/Red/Blue; Orange/Green/Red; Orange/Green/Blue
b) Pink/Green